ESSENTIAL DK COMPUTERS

SPREADSHEETS

FORMATTING & PRINTING

ABOUT THIS BOOK

Formatting & Printing is for people who already have a basic understanding of Microsoft's Excel 2000 spreadsheet program, including opening a new worksheet, entering data, and saving.

EXCEL'S COMPREHENSIVE FEATURES FOR designing and manipulating spreadsheets are far from being the end of the story. The program also incorporates sophisticated formatting and printing capabilities that are presented here in separate chapters to allow an easy understanding of their functions.

The chapters and the subsections present the information using step-by-step sequences. Virtually every step is accompanied by an illustration showing how your screen should look at each stage.

The book assumes that you know how to enter data into a worksheet; how to change or correct this data; how to copy and move data around the worksheet; and how to insert, clear, and delete cells. The bulk of this book concentrates on the wide range of formatting options that can be applied to the different kinds of data that Excel is able to manipulate. These options include different levels of text formatting and the many ways in which numerical data can be formatted, such as currency amounts and dates. Some basic examples run through the book, and it may be difficult to keep track

This book is designed for anyone who wants to improve the appearance, clarity, and design of their worksheets

of these if you skip any sections. (Note: these examples are designed to illustrate various specific techniques, and do not necessarily reflect typical worksheet uses.) The book contains several features to help you understand both what is happening and what you need to do. A labeled Excel window is included to show you where to find the important elements in Excel. This is followed by an illustration of the rows of buttons, or *toolbars*, at the top of the screen, to help you find your way around these controls.

Command keys, such as ENTER and CTRL, are shown in these rectangles: [Enter ←] and [Ctrl], so that there's no confusion, for example, over whether you should press that key, or type the letters "ctrl".

Cross-references are shown in the text as left- or right-hand page icons: ◁ and ▷. The page number and the reference are shown at the foot of the page.

As well as the step-by-step sections, there are boxes that explain a feature in detail, and tip boxes that provide alternative methods and shortcuts. Finally, at the back, you will find a glossary explaining new terms, and a comprehensive index.

ESSENTIAL **DK** COMPUTERS
S P R E A D S H E E T S

FORMATTING & PRINTING

S U E   E T H E R I N G T O N

A Dorling Kindersley Book

Dorling Kindersley
LONDON, NEW YORK, DELHI, SYDNEY,
PARIS, MUNICH, JOHANNESBURG

Produced for Dorling Kindersley Limited by
Design Revolution, Queens Park Villa,
30 West Drive, Brighton, East Sussex BN2 2GE

EDITORIAL DIRECTOR Ian Whitelaw
SENIOR DESIGNER Andy Ashdown
PROJECT EDITOR John Watson
DESIGNER Andrew Easton

MANAGING EDITOR Sharon Lucas
SENIOR MANAGING ART EDITOR Derek Coombes
DTP DESIGNER Sonia Charbonnier
PRODUCTION CONTROLLER Wendy Penn

Published in Great Britain in 2000 by
Dorling Kindersley Limited,
9 Henrietta Street, London WC2E 8PS

2 4 6 8 10 9 7 5 3 1

A CIP catalog record for this book is available from the British Library.

ISBN 0-7513-0998-2

Color reproduced by First Impressions, London
Printed in Italy by Graphicom

For our complete
catalog visit
www.dk.com

CONTENTS

MICROSOFT EXCEL

Excel belongs to the group of computer applications known as spreadsheets, and the first spreadsheet program started the process of making computers an indispensable business tool.

WHAT CAN EXCEL DO?

Storing spreadsheet data is only the beginning as far as Excel is concerned. The wide range of features it contains lets you manipulate and present your data in almost any way you choose. Excel can be an accounts program; it can be used as a sophisticated calculator capable of utilizing complex mathematical formulas; it can also be a diary, a scheduler, and more. Used in combination with Microsoft Word, Excel's database features make creating mailing lists and personalized letters very easy. Excel's presentation facilities use color, borders, and different fonts to emphasize data. A variety of charts is available, which can be selected to suit the kind of data being presented. For storing, manipulating, and presenting data, Microsoft Excel offers an unrivaled range of possibilities.

WHAT IS A WORKSHEET?

At the heart of Excel is a two-dimensional grid of data storage spaces called a worksheet (right). This is where you input the data that you want to store, manipulate, or analyze. The individual spaces are called worksheet cells. To begin with, all the cells are empty. As you put data into the cells, you build and develop the individual worksheets.

LAUNCHING EXCEL

Approaching a new program for the first time can be a daunting experience because you don't know what to expect. However, new programs are learned one step at a time and the first step is the simple one of launching Excel from your desktop.

1 LAUNCHING WITH THE START MENU

● If you are running Windows 95 or 98, click on the **Start** button at bottom left, and then choose **Programs** from the pop-up list. Microsoft Excel should appear in the submenu to the right (or it may be within a Microsoft Office Program group). Highlight the words **Microsoft Excel** and click with the mouse.
● The Excel window appears on screen ⌐.

2 LAUNCHING WITH A SHORTCUT

● If there is already a shortcut to Excel on your Desktop, just double-click on the shortcut icon.
● The Excel window appears on screen ⌐.

The Excel Window

THE EXCEL WINDOW

Soon after you launch Microsoft Excel, a window called **Microsoft Excel – Book1** appears. At the center of the window is a worksheet – a grid of blank rectangular cells. Letters and numbers label the columns and rows of the grid. Each cell has an address (such as E3), which is the column and row in which it is found.

THE EXCEL WINDOW

1 Title bar
Title of the active workbook.

2 Menu bar
Contains the main menus for frequently used commands.

3 Formula bar
What you enter in the active cell also appears here.

4 Standard toolbar
These buttons carry out frequently used actions.

5 Formatting toolbar
Options for changing data presentation.

6 Column header buttons
Click on the header button to select the whole column.

7 Row header buttons
Click on the row header to select the entire row.

8 Active cell
Whatever you type appears in the active cell.

9 Worksheet tabs
Workbooks contain worksheets – click to select one.

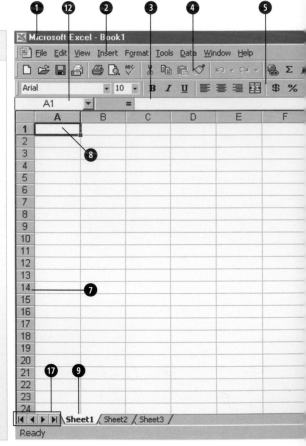

TOOLBAR LAYOUT

If Excel doesn't show the Formatting toolbar below the Standard toolbar, first place the cursor over the Formatting toolbar "handle." When the four-headed arrow appears, (right) hold down the mouse button and "drag" the toolbar into position.

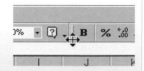

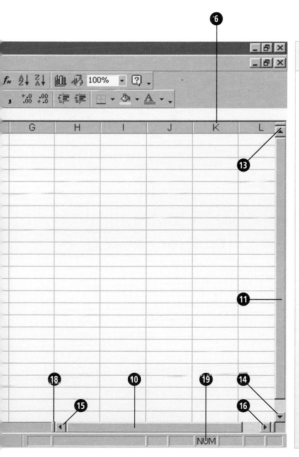

THE EXCEL WINDOW

⓾ Horizontal scroll bar
To scroll horizontally through the worksheet.

⓫ Vertical scroll bar
To scroll vertically through the worksheet.

⓬ Name box
Gives the address of the active cell.

⓭ Scroll-up arrow
Move up the worksheet.

⓮ Scroll-down arrow
Move down the worksheet.

⓯ Left-scroll arrow
Scrolls the sheet to the left.

⓰ Right-scroll arrow
Scrolls the sheet to the right.

⓱ Tab scrolling buttons
Scroll through the sheets if they cannot all be displayed.

⓲ Tab split box
Click and drag to show tabs or to increase the scroll bar.

⓳ NUM lock
Shows that the numeric keypad on the right of the keyboard is on.

THE TWO MAIN EXCEL TOOLBARS

Many of the actions, or commands, that you want to perform on data can be carried out by clicking on toolbar buttons. When you launch Excel, the Standard toolbar and the Formatting toolbar are the usual toolbars displayed. They contain buttons whose actions are described below. The Standard toolbar contains buttons for actions as diverse as opening a new workbook or undoing an action. The Formatting toolbar contains buttons for changing the worksheet's appearance.

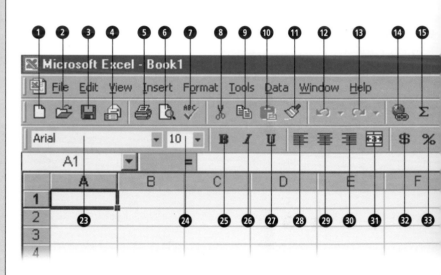

BUTTON FUNCTIONS

1. New workbook
2. Open file
3. Save workbook
4. Email workbook/sheet
5. Print
6. Print preview ⌐
7. Spelling checker
8. Cut
9. Copy
10. Paste
11. Format painter
12. Undo action(s)
13. Redo action(s)
14. Insert hyperlink
15. AutoSum
16. Paste function
17. Sort ascending
18. Sort descending
19. Chart wizard
20. Drawing toolbar ⌐
21. Zoom view ⌐
22. Help
23. Font selector
24. Font size selector

| 44 | Print preview |

| 66 | The drawing toolbar |

| 44 | The zoom button |

CUSTOMIZING A TOOLBAR

Click the arrow at far right of the Formatting toolbar then on the arrow on the Add or Remove Buttons box that appears. A drop-down menu opens from which you can add or remove toolbar buttons.

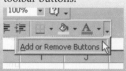

ScreenTips
It isn't necessary to memorize all these buttons. Roll the cursor over a button, wait for a second, and a ScreenTip appears telling you the function of the button.

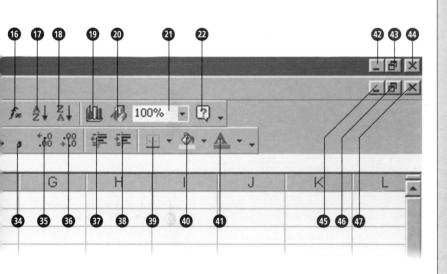

BUTTON FUNCTIONS

- ⑮ Bold
- ⑯ Italic
- ⑰ Underline
- ⑱ Align left
- ⑲ Center
- ⑳ Align right
- ㉑ Merge and center
- ㉒ Currency style
- ㉝ Percent style
- ㉞ Comma style
- ㉟ Increase decimals
- ㊱ Decrease decimals
- ㊲ Decrease indent
- ㊳ Increase indent
- ㊴ Add/remove borders
- ㊵ Fill color
- ㊶ Font color
- ㊷ Minimize Excel
- ㊸ Restore Excel
- ㊹ Close Excel
- ㊺ Minimize worksheet
- ㊻ Restore worksheet
- ㊼ Close worksheet

| 20 | Entering commas | 21 | Decimal places | 36 | Applying the fill color |

NAMING, SAVING, AND FINDING WORKBOOKS

Anything you create using Microsoft Excel is stored on your computer as a file called a workbook. A workbook contains one or more separate worksheets. When you first start up Excel, you are presented with an unused workbook called Book1. This contains from three to ten blank worksheets, depending on the version of Excel. The blank worksheets are initially called Sheet1, Sheet2, and so on.

1 RENAMING A WORKSHEET

● You can switch between worksheets by clicking on the tabs at the bottom of the workbook window. To begin with, the worksheets are all blank.

● Once you put data into a worksheet, you can give the worksheet a short name to indicate what it contains. Because all worksheets start with a default name (like Sheet1), you are actually renaming the worksheet. Here's how to do it.

● Double-click on the existing name, so that it becomes highlighted.

● Type the new name and press [Enter ←].

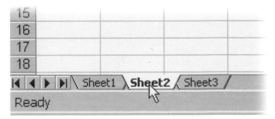

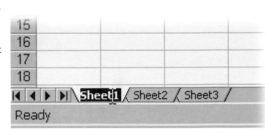

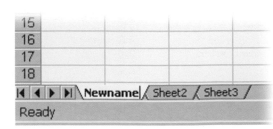

2 SAVING AND NAMING

You should save your work frequently. Saving means copying to your computer's hard disk. When you save in Excel, you save the whole workbook containing the worksheet(s) that you have been developing.

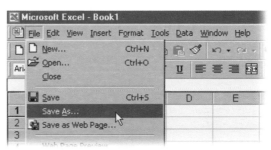

● The first time you save a workbook, you can name it (actually rename it) at the same time.

● Choose **Save As** from the **File** menu.

● The **Save As** dialog box appears. Your workbook will be saved in the folder displayed in the **Save in** box. In this instance, just accept the displayed folder. Remember the name of the folder in which you've saved the workbook.

● In the **File name** box, type the name you would like to give your workbook (Excel will automatically add the extension **.xls**). Then click on the **Save** button.

● On subsequent occasions when you want to save the workbook, just click the **Save** button on the Standard toolbar.

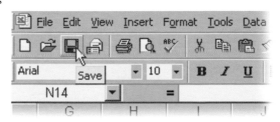

3 CLOSING A WORKBOOK

- Click the **Close Window** button at top right.
- If you have made any changes since you last saved, a box appears asking whether you want to save changes. Click **Yes** (or **No** if you do not wish to save any changes you've made).

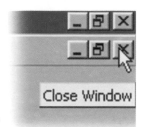

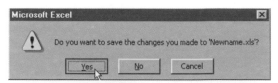

4 OPENING A NEW WORKBOOK

- Just click the **New** workbook button on the Standard toolbar.

5 OPEN A SAVED WORKBOOK

- Click the **Open** button on the Standard toolbar
- In the **Open** dialog box, click on the workbook you want to open.
- Click on the **Open** button at bottom right of the box.

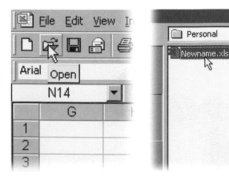

6 FIND A SAVED WORKBOOK

● After you have been using Excel for some time, there will be occasions when you cannot find the workbook you want. Excel contains its own find-file facility to help when this happens.

● To find a workbook, begin by clicking on **Open** in the **File** menu, click on **Tools** at top right in the **Open** dialog box, and choose **Find**.

● The **Find** dialog box opens. Drop down the **Look in:** menu and select the area to search – in this case, the folder called My Documents. Click in the **Search subfolders** check box if necessary, and click on **Find now**.

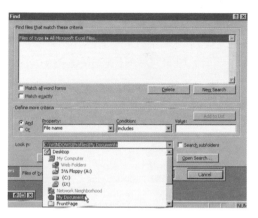

● The **Open** dialog box reappears with the list of Excel workbooks that have been found.

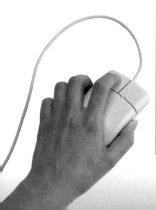

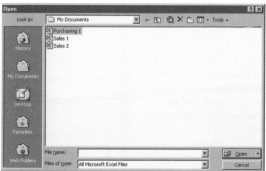

FORMATTING DATA

There are four types of data that can be input into an Excel worksheet – text, numbers, dates, and formulas. We begin by looking at the formatting of the first three.

DIFFERENT DATA – DIFFERENT FORMATS

Each cell in a worksheet has a *format* associated with it. On a new worksheet, every cell has the format called *General*, which is the format used for cells containing text. However, when, for example, a currency amount is entered in a cell and a currency format applied, the cell retains that format until the cell's format is changed. This is true for all types of formatting when applied to a cell. The example used here concerns the different types of desserts included on the menu at the South Lodge Hotel. The data is held in an Excel table and includes the name of the dessert, the number of desserts sold over a year, the cost and percentage profit for each dessert, and the date the dessert costs are to be recalculated.

1 TITLE AND COLUMN HEADS

● Launch the Excel program so that you have a new worksheet on your screen.

Old versions of Excel
If you have worksheets created with an earlier version of Excel, Excel 2000 can handle all the data, formatting, and formulas they contain.

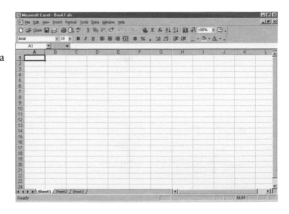

● Click on the cell A2 and enter the title of the table: **SOUTH LODGE HOTEL DESSERTS**. Don't worry that the text overflows into columns B, C, and D – this will be corrected later.

● Click on cell A4 and enter the column heading **Dessert name** in upper- and lower-case letters.

● Use the [Tab⇆] key, first to move to column B, and then to subsequent columns to enter the following headings:
Column B – **Desserts sold**
Column C – **Cost per dessert**
Column D – **% profit**
Column E – **Date next costed**

● Press [Enter←] at the end of the last heading.

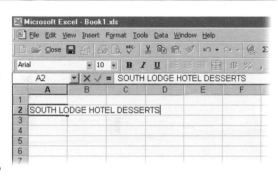

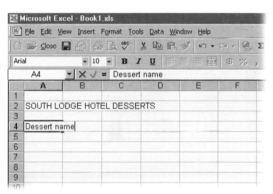

2 COLUMN AUTOFIT

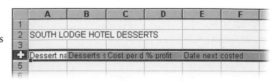

● It is immediately obvious that some of the column headings are too long for the width of the column. Excel has a command that widens the columns to fit the text.

● Select row 4.

● Click on **Format** on the Menu bar, then on **Column,** and finally on **AutoFit Selection.**

● The headings are now shown in full.

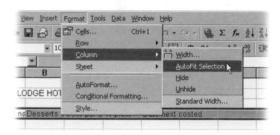

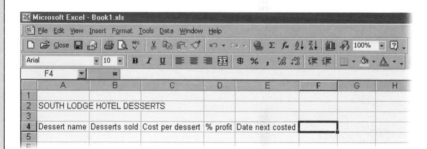

3 ENTERING THE DESSERT NAMES

● The dessert names are now to be entered in column A beginning on row 6. The desserts names are: **Blackberry & Apple Crumble Banoffee Pie Fresh Fruit Salad Pecan Pie Chocolate Sponge**.

4 ENTERING NUMBERS

● Click on cell B6 and enter the number of Blackberry & Apple Crumbles sold: **11245**.
● Press the Enter← key and Excel automatically takes you to cell B7.

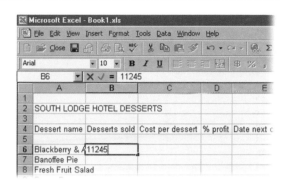

● Continue entering the numbers as shown on the example and press the Enter← key after entering the last number.

	A	B	C	D	E
1					
2	SOUTH LODGE HOTEL DESSERTS				
3					
4	Dessert name	Desserts sold	Cost per dessert	% profit	Date next c
5					
6	Blackberry & A	11245			
7	Danoffee Pie	10541			
8	Fresh Fruit Sal	22341			
9	Pecan Pie	12697			
10	Chocolate Spo	9234			
11					
12					

ENTERING COMMAS

● Where the numbers of desserts sold is greater than 999, we wish to format the numbers with commas to indicate the numbers in thousands. This makes the numbers easier to read.

● Select the cells B6 to B9.

● Click on the **Comma Style** icon on the formatting toolbar.

● The numbers of desserts sold now have a comma after each third digit.

NUMBER FORMATS

There are many built-in number formats contained within Excel. To see them, click on **Format**, choose **Cells**, and click on the **Number** tab. The formats are organized into categories, which are listed down the left-hand side of the **Categories** box.

Comma inserted in five-digit numbers ●

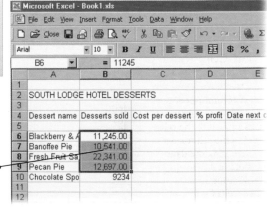

5 DECIMAL PLACES

● As part of the standard comma style, the numbers of desserts sold have two decimal places. As it is not possible to sell a fraction of a dessert, the decimal places need to be removed.

● With the cells still selected, click on the **Decrease Decimal** button twice – one click for each decimal place to be removed from the total.

● The numbers now have no decimal places.

More decimals

The **Increase Decimal** is similar to the **Decrease Decimal** button except that for every click a decimal place is added to the number format

	A	B	C	D	E
1					
2	SOUTH LODGE HOTEL DESSERTS				
3					
4	Dessert name	Desserts sold	Cost per dessert	% profit	Date next c
5					
6	Blackberry & A	11,245			
7	Banoffee Pie	10,541			
8	Fresh Fruit Sal	22,341			
9	Pecan Pie	12,697			
10	Chocolate Spo	9234			
11					
12					
13					
14					
15					
16					

6 FORMATTING THE CURRENCY

● The currency figures are to be entered in dollars in the next column, **Cost per dessert**, and the currency format applied to the cells. Changing the cell format before entering the data means that a dollar sign is inserted automatically.

● Select cells C6 to C10.

	A	B	C	D	E
1					
2	SOUTH LODGE HOTEL DESSERTS				
3					
4	Dessert name	Desserts sold	Cost per dessert	% profit	Date next c
5					
6	Blackberry & A	11,245			
7	Banoffee Pie	10,541			
8	Fresh Fruit Sal	22,341			
9	Pecan Pie	12,697			
10	Chocolate Spo	9234			
11					
12					
13					
14					
15					

● Click on **Format** on the Menu bar and select **Cells**.

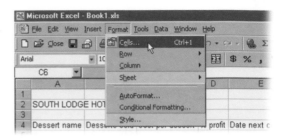

● The **Format Cells** dialog box opens. Click on the **Number** tab at the top of the dialog box and choose **Currency** from the **Category:** list.

● As we need two decimal places for our currency amounts, we can leave the **Decimal places** box set to 2. Click on **OK** at the bottom of the dialog box.

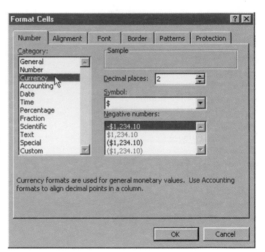

● Click on cell B6 and enter the amount **0.75** and press [Enter ←]. Notice that the dollar sign is inserted automatically in front of the number.

Dollar sign is inserted automatically ●

• Continue entering the amounts as shown in the example, pressing [Enter←] after each amount.

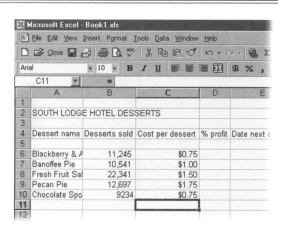

7 PERCENTAGE FUNCTION

• The % (percentage) function in Excel automatically multiplies the number in the cell by 100 and places the % sign after the figure. Thus, if the % amount is 20%, you need only enter **0.2** and then use the % function. Let's enter the Profit amounts in column D.

• Click on cell D6 and enter the number **5** and then press [Enter←].

• Complete the rest of the figures as shown in the example.

● Select the cells from D6 to D10.

● Click on the % button on the toolbar.

● The numbers in the column have now been reformatted as percentages.

Percentage button ●

YOUR CURRENCY

You are not limited to the dollar sign as the currency symbol in Excel. If you want Excel always to use another currency symbol, open the **Regional Settings** properties dialog box from the **Control Panel** and click the **Currency** tab to select an alternative currency.

8 ENTERING DATES

● When you enter a date in the format *mm/dd/yy* (where *mm* is the month, *dd* is the day, and *yy* is the last two digits of the year), Excel recognizes this as a date and the cell's format is converted automatically to the date format.

● Click on the cell E6 and enter the date **4/1/00** and press [Enter ↵].

● Continue to enter the other dates in cells E7 to E10 as shown in the worked example.

● We have now set up and formatted the basic table of data on our Excel worksheet.

● The next section of the book deals with further formatting applied to the texts and dates in the table.

Microsoft Excel - Book1.xls

File Edit View Insert Format Tools Data Window Help

	A	B	C	D	E
1					
2	SOUTH LODGE HOTEL DESSERTS				
3					
4	Dessert name	Desserts sold	Cost per dessert	% profit	Date next costed
5					
6	Blackberry & A	11,245	$0.75	500%	4/1/00
7	Banoffee Pie	10,541	$1.00	450%	
8	Fresh Fruit Sal	22,341	$1.50	700%	
9	Pecan Pie	12,697	$1.75	186%	
10	Chocolate Spo	9234	$0.75	300%	
11					
12					
13					
14					

Microsoft Excel - Book1.xls

File Edit View Insert Format Tools Data Window Help

	A	B	C	D	E
1					
2	SOUTH LODGE HOTEL DESSERTS				
3					
4	Dessert name	Desserts sold	Cost per dessert	% profit	Date next costed
5					
6	Blackberry & A	11,245	$0.75	500%	4/1/00
7	Banoffee Pie	10,541	$1.00	450%	5/1/00
8	Fresh Fruit Sal	22,341	$1.50	700%	4/2/00
9	Pecan Pie	12,697	$1.75	186%	12/20/01
10	Chocolate Spo	9234	$0.75	300%	11/20/01
11					
12					
13					
14					
15					
16					

Two-digit years

When you enter two-digit year dates, Excel 2000 interprets "00" to "29" as being "2000" to "2029." The years "30" to "99" are interpreted as "1930" to "1999."

TEXT AND DATES

The majority of tables that you create using Excel will contain titles, headings, or dates. When these are well laid out, they give the data a more professional look and are easier to read.

REFORMATTING THE SECTIONS

We now need to start formatting the title and headings in the table so that they stand out from the rest of the data. Let's reformat each part of the table as necessary, starting with the title. Also, although we can see the column headings in full, some of the dessert names are still hidden behind column B.

1 MERGING CELLS

- The title SOUTH LODGE HOTEL DESSERTS is contained in cell A2 but overflows into columns B and C. The title needs to be in a larger, bold font, and centered above the table so that it stands out from the remainder of the text.

- The first step is to use the **Merge** command, which merges two or more cells into one. Begin by selecting the cells A2 to E2.

	A	B	C	D	E
1					
2	SOUTH LODGE HOTEL DESSERTS				
3					
4	Dessert name	Desserts sold	Cost per dessert	% profit	Date next costed
5					
6	Blackberry & A	11,245	$0.75	500%	4/1/00
7	Banoffee Pie	10,541	$1.00	450%	5/1/00
8	Fresh Fruit Sal	22,341	$1.50	700%	4/2/00
9	Pecan Pie	12,697	$1.75	186%	12/20/01
10	Chocolate Spo	9234	$0.75	300%	11/20/01
11					
12					
13					

Splitting merged cells
To change a merged cell back to separate cells, highlight the cell, click Cells on the **Format** menu, and clear the **Merged cells** check box in the Alignment tab.

● Click on **Format** in the
Menu bar and choose **Cells**.
● The **Format Cells** dialog
box opens. Click on the
Alignment tab at the top of
the box.
● Click in the **Merge cells**
check box and click on **OK**.

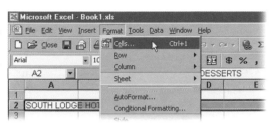

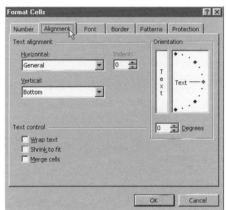

● The five cells, A2–E2, are
now merged into one
extended cell.

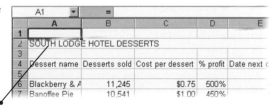

Five cells merged into one

● With the new extended cell selected, click on the **Bold**, **Underline**, and **Center** buttons in sequence and the title is now much more prominent.

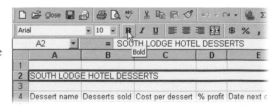

Font coloring

It's also possible to change the font color, particularly to emphasize a title. First highlight the text, and click the **Font Color** button 🔲 on the Formatting toolbar to apply the most recently used color. Click the arrow next to the button to see a palette of colors from which to choose.

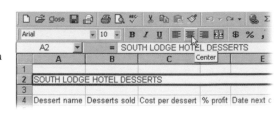

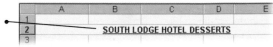

Text is now clearly a title ●

2 FORMAT COLUMN HEADINGS

● The headings also need to be given greater prominence so that they stand out from the data below them and the data held in the table. Select cells A4 to E4.

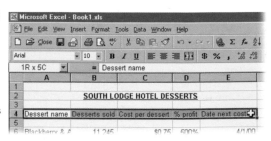

• Click on the down arrow next to the Font box on the Formatting menu, scroll down the list of fonts that are available and click on **Times New Roman**.

• Click on the down arrow next to the Font size box and choose **12**.

• Click on the **Bold** button on the Formatting toolbar to make the headings bold.

• The headings are now looking better, but still require further formatting.

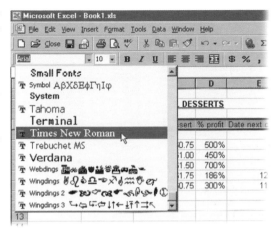

3 TEXT WRAPPING

• As the format of the headings has changed, they are too wide for the columns. The table would look better if the heading texts were *wrapped* in each heading cell.

• With the headings still selected click on **Format** on the Menu bar, select **Cells**, and click on the **Alignment** tab at the top of the **Format Cells** dialog box.

• Click on the **Wrap text** check box at the foot of the dialog box.

• Click on **OK**. The headings are wrapped in the column heading cells.

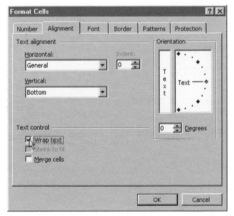

4 CENTERING TEXT

● The headings would look better if they were centered in the column cells. With the headings still selected, click on the **Center** button on the Formatting toolbar, and click anywhere on the worksheet to deselect the cells. The headings are centered in the columns.

Wrapped and centered headings   *Center button*

5 AUTOFITTING TEXT

● Now we have completed the formatting of the title and the headings of the table. However, you can see that some of the dessert names are still not shown in full. There are several ways to change the column width, but this time let's use the column **AutoFit** function again ⌐.

● Select the table of data, cells A4 to E10.

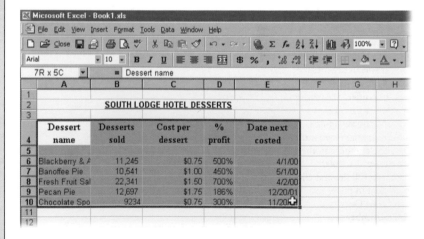

• Click on **Format** in the Menu bar, select **Columns**, and **Autofit Selection**.
• The dessert names are now clearly visible.

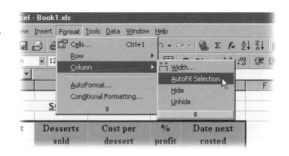

	A	B	C	D	E
1					
2	**SOUTH LODGE HOTEL DESSERTS**				
3					
4	**Dessert name**	Desserts sold	Cost per dessert	% profit	Date n(coste
5					
6	Blackberry & Apple Crumble	11,245	$0.75	500%	4/1
7	Banoffee Pie	10,541	$1.00	450%	5/1
8	Fresh Fruit Salad	22,341	$1.50	700%	4/2
9	Pecan Pie	12,697	$1.75	186%	12/20
10	Chocolate Sponge	9234	$0.75	300%	11/20
11					
12					
13					

6 FORMATTING DATES

• When we first input the dates, it was in the format *mm/dd/yy*. However, there are many different formats available in Excel from which to choose. For our working example, we want the dates to appear in the format: April 1, 2000.
• Click in cell E6, and click on **Format** in the Menu bar, choose **Cells**, and click on the **Number** tab.

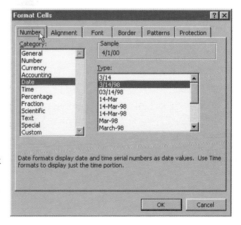

● The **Date** category is already highlighted. In the **Type** section, an example is also highlighted. The **Sample** box shows the date in the table in E6 as 4/1/00. Scroll down the different **Types** and click on one to see the date 4/1/00 in the **Sample** box.

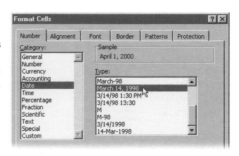

● The format we require is shown as March 14, 1998, which you can see is displayed in the **Sample** box as April 1, 2000.

● Click on **OK** at the bottom of the dialog box. The cell where the date should appear in the table may be filled with hash signs. In Excel this means that the cell is not large enough to show the newly formatted data. The column needs to be widened.

● With the cell still selected, click on **Format**, choose **Column** and click on **Autofit Selection** ⌐. The column is now sufficiently wide to display the date.

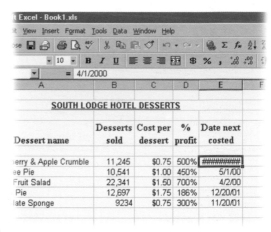

SOUTH LODGE HOTEL DESSERTS

Dessert name	Desserts sold	Cost per dessert	% profit	Date next costed
erry & Apple Crumble	11,245	$0.75	500%	#########
ee Pie	10,541	$1.00	450%	5/1/00
Fruit Salad	22,341	$1.50	700%	4/2/00
Pie	12,697	$1.75	186%	12/20/01
late Sponge	9234	$0.75	300%	11/20/01

SOUTH LODGE HOTEL DESSERTS

Dessert name	Desserts sold	Cost per dessert	% profit	Date next costed
erry & Apple Crumble	11,245	$0.75	500%	April 1, 2000
e Pie	10,541	$1.00	450%	5/1/00
ruit Salad	22,341	$1.50	700%	4/2/00
Pie	12,697	$1.75	186%	12/20/01
ate Sponge	9234	$0.75	300%	11/20/01

| 18 | **Column AutoFit** |

7 USING FORMAT PAINTER

● Now we have set up the first date in the format of our choice, we need to reformat the other dates. An easy way to do this is to use **Format Painter** on the Standard toolbar.

● Click on the formatted date in E6 and click on the **Format Painter** button.

● As you move the cursor onto the worksheet a small paintbrush is now attached to it. Move the cursor to cell E7 and, holding down the mouse button, drag the cursor over the four remaining dates.

● Release the mouse button and the newly formatted dates that fit in the column are displayed in full. The longer dates can be fitted by using the **Autofit Selection** command (see opposite), after which all the dates are displayed.

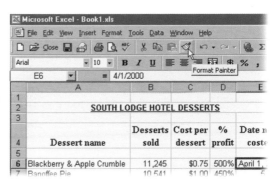

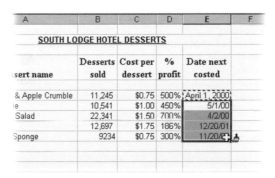

The dates are shown in full ●

BORDERS AND COLORS

In addition to formatting the text, there are other features
contained within Excel 2000 to enhance the appearance of your
tables. Different border styles and colors are easy to use.

CHOOSING BORDERS AND COLORS

To give Excel tables more impact you can
easily apply borders and colors to them.
This section shows you how to apply
different border styles, fill the
backgrounds with different colors, and
change the font colors of texts and
numbers. AutoFormat is then introduced
as a method of using Excel's own formats.

1 APPLYING BORDERS

● We'll start by applying a
border to the entire table
manually. Select the whole
table, cells A1 to E10, and
click on the down arrow to
the right of the **Borders**
button on the Formatting
toolbar. From the options
on the menu choose the
Thick Box Border.

● Click anywhere on the worksheet to deselect the table. The right-side and bottom borders can be seen, but the borders along the top and left-side of the table are not visible. However, they are present and will be printed out.

	A	B	C	D	E	F	G
1							
2		SOUTH LODGE HOTEL DESSERTS					
3							
4	Dessert name	Desserts sold	Cost per dessert	% profit	Date next costed		
5							
6	Blackberry & Apple Crumble	11,245	$0.75	500%	April 1, 2000		
7	Banoffee Pie	10,541	$1.00	450%	May 1, 2000		
8	Fresh Fruit Salad	22,341	$1.50	700%	April 2, 2000		
9	Pecan Pie	12,697	$1.75	186%	December 20, 2001		
10	Chocolate Sponge	9234	$0.75	300%	November 20, 2001		
11							
12							

	A	B	C	D	E	F	G
1							
2		SOUTH LODGE HOTEL DESSERTS					
3							
4	Dessert name	Desserts sold	Cost per dessert	% profit	Date next costed		
5							
6	Blackberry & Apple Crumble	11,245	$0.75	500%	April 1, 2000		
7	Banoffee Pie	10,541	$1.00	450%	May 1, 2000		
8	Fresh Fruit Salad	22,341	$1.50	700%	April 2, 2000		
9	Pecan Pie	12,697	$1.75	186%	December 20, 2001		
10	Chocolate Sponge	9234	$0.75	300%	November 20, 2001		
11							
12							

● To apply a border to the headings, begin by selecting the cells A4 to E4.
● Click on the down arrow to the right of the **Borders** button, but this time choose the **Top and Double Bottom Border**.

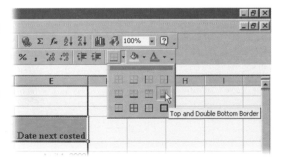

● To border the desserts name column select cells A5 to A10.

● Click on the borders icon as before and choose the **Right Border**.

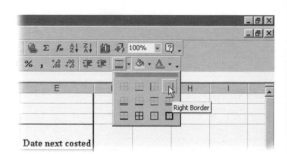

2 APPLYING THE FILL COLOR

● With the cells still selected, some background color can be added to the dessert names.

● Click on the down arrow next to the **Fill Color** button ⬜ on the Formatting toolbar. In our example, we have chosen yellow.

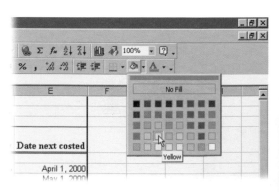

● Select the top of the table
(cells A1 to E4) and using
the **Fill Color** button as
before, select **Light Yellow**.

Microsoft Excel - Book1

File Edit View Insert Format Tools Data Window Help

Times New Roman ▾ 12 ▾ **B** *I* <u>U</u> ≡ ≡ ≡ ≣ $ % , ⁰⁰⁸ ⁰⁸ 律 律 ▦ ▾ ◊ ▾ **A** ▾ ▾

E4 = Date next costed

No Fill

Light Yellow

	A	B	C	D	E	F
1						
2	SOUTH LODGE HOTEL DESSERTS					
3						
4	Dessert name	Desserts sold	Cost per dessert	% profit	Date next costed	
5						
6	Blackberry & Apple Crumble	11,245	$0.75	500%	April 1, 2000	
7	Banoffee Pie	10,541	$1.00	450%	May 1, 2000	
8	Fresh Fruit Salad	22,341	$1.50	700%	April 2, 2000	
9	Pecan Pie	12,697	$1.75	186%	December 20, 2001	
10	Chocolate Sponge	9234	$0.75	300%	November 20, 2001	
11						
12						
13						

3 APPLYING FONT COLOR

● To make the dessert
names stand out even
more, we can change the
color of their font.

● Select cells A6 to A10.

Microsoft Excel - Book1

File Edit View Insert Format Tools Data Window Help

Arial ▾ 10 ▾ **B** *I* <u>U</u> ≡ ≡ ≡ ≣ $ % , ⁰⁰⁸ ⁰⁸

A5 =

	A	B	C	D	E
1					
2	SOUTH LODGE HOTEL DESSERTS				
3					
4	Dessert name	Desserts sold	Cost per dessert	% profit	Date next cost
5					
6	Blackberry & Apple Crumble	11,245	$0.75	500%	April 1, 20
7	Banoffee Pie	10,541	$1.00	450%	May 1, 20
8	Fresh Fruit Salad	22,341	$1.50	700%	April 2, 20
9	Pecan Pie	12,697	$1.75	186%	December 20, 20
10	Chocolate Sponge	9234	$0.75	300%	November 20, 20
11					
12					
13					
14					
15					
16					
17					

● Click on the down arrow next to the **Font Color** icon on the Formatting toolbar.

● Click on the color **Plum**.

● Click off the table to see the effect of the colored text. We have now completed the formatting of our table and it is ready to print out.

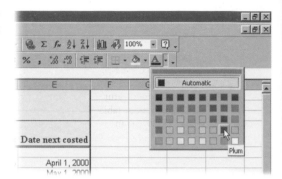

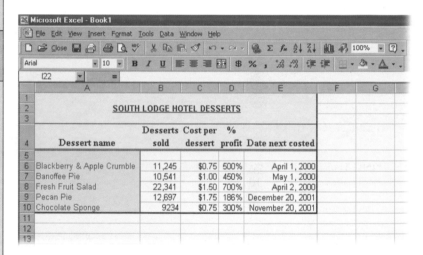

CHANGING THE AVAILABLE COLORS

You can alter the range of colors displayed on the palette. From the **Tools** menu select **Options** and click the **Color** tab of the **Options** dialog box. Click on one of the **Standard colors** that you wish to alter and click on **Modify**. The **Colors** dialog box opens showing a hexagon-shaped collection of colors. As you click on a color, a square panel to the right shows the color that you clicked on as the Current color and above it is the new color you have selected.

USING AUTOFORMAT

Although we have designed the South Lodge Hotel Desserts table ourselves, you can also use the AutoFormat feature of Excel to apply a design to your table of data quickly and easily. When an AutoFormat style is applied to any Excel data, the existing formatting style is erased and replaced with the selected design. As we wish to print our existing table later, let's make a copy of our table and use the copy to look at the different formatting options in AutoFormat.

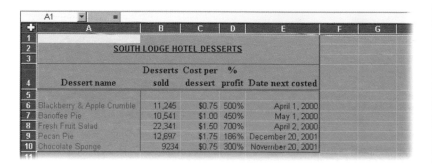

COPYING THE TABLE

• Select the table, cells A1 to E10.

• Click on the **Copy** button on the Standard toolbar.

• You will see that the table has a moving dotted line around it, called a marquee.

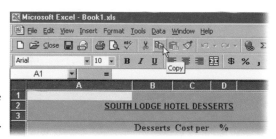

Selection errors
If you have accidentally selected and copied some cells in error, press the [Esc] key to remove the marquee and then make another selection of the correct cells.

● Click on Sheet2 at the bottom of your screen. Cell A1 is already selected.

● Click on the **Paste** button on the Standard toolbar.

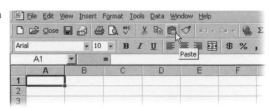

● You can see that the copied table is smaller than the original. The column **AutoFit Selection** can be used again to make the columns wide enough to fit the data. The copied table is still selected so we don't need to select it again.

● Click on **Format**, followed by **Column** and then **AutoFit Selection**.

	A	B	C	D	E	F
1						
2		SOUTH LODGE HOTEL DESSERTS				
3						
4	Dessert name	Dessert s sold	Cost per dessert	% profit	Date next costed	
5						
6	Blackberry	11,245	$0.75	500%	########	
7	Banoffee F	10,541	$1.00	450%	########	
8	Fresh Fruit	22,341	$1.50	700%	########	
9	Pecan Pie	12,697	$1.75	186%	########	
10	Chocolate	9234	$0.75	300%	########	
11						
12						
13						

Remove AutoFormat
To remove AutoFormat, select the cells that have been autoformatted. In the **Format** menu choose **AutoFormat**, scroll to the end of the list in the **AutoFormat** dialog box and click on the **None** option.

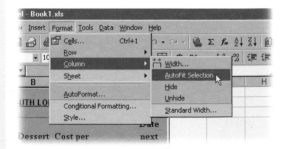

ADJUSTING THE COLUMN MANUALLY

● Column B is too narrow, but can be made wider by using the same method as used in formatting the dates . Place the mouse cursor over the line between columns B and C. The cursor becomes a double-headed black arrow. Hold down the left mouse button and drag the cursor to the right.

● Release the mouse button and the column title is displayed in full.

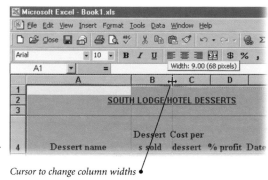

Cursor to change column widths ●

Column heading now fits ●

AUTOFORMAT

● Now we can use the **AutoFormat** feature of Excel 2000. Click on **Format** on the Menu bar, followed by **AutoFormat**.

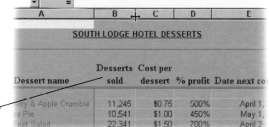

| 31 | **Formatting dates** |

● The **AutoFormat** dialog box opens. AutoFormat offers 17 styles of table format that display the data in various ways.

● Scroll down through the styles until **List 1** is shown.
● Click on the **List 1** style. It is enclosed within a black border. Each format has

options associated with it, which can be seen by clicking on **Options** at the top right of the **AutoFormat** dialog box.

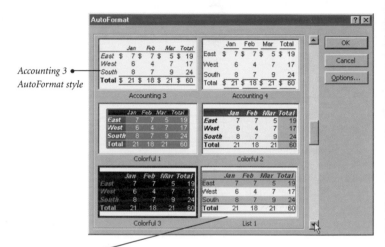

Accounting 3 AutoFormat style

List 1 Autoformat style

Options button for more choices

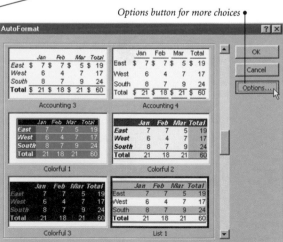

● The Options panel opens at the foot of the Auto-Format dialog box and are named **Formats to apply**.

● All the options are initially applied to the chosen style. If you do not want an option applied, click in the relevant check box to deselect it and the changes are reflected in the sample boxes. However, not all options apply to every format style.

● These default settings can all be applied to the table simply by clicking **OK**.

● The dialog box closes and the new format style is applied to the worksheet.

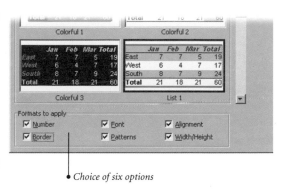

Choice of six options

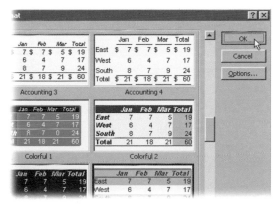

PAGE SETUP TO PRINT

The page setup options in Excel give you a great deal of control over your table's printed appearance. These range from positioning the table on the page to adding surrounding text.

CHOOSING THE OPTIONS

We have formatted our Excel table of data on the screen and now we want to print the Sheet1 copy. Before printing in Excel there are several steps to be completed. The first step is to look at your Excel table using **Print Preview**. This shows exactly how your Excel table will appear on the printed page. From this view you can decide whether you want to make any changes without wasting paper.

1 PRINT PREVIEW

● Click on **Print Preview** on the Standard toolbar to see how the table would look on the printed page.
● Click on **Zoom** at the top of the Print Preview window, to see your table in more detail.

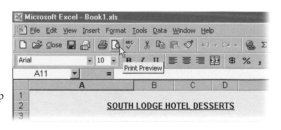

The Zoom Button

The Zoom button is called a toggle button (similar to an on/off switch), and you can zoom in and out of the page as many times as you like.

SOUTH LODGE HOTEL DESSERTS				
Dessert name	Desserts sold	Cost per dessert	% profit	Date next costed
Blackberry & Apple Crumble	11,245	$0.75	500%	April 1, 2000
Banoffee Pie	10,541	$1.00	450%	May 1, 2000
Fresh Fruit Salad	22,341	$1.50	700%	April 2, 2000
Pecan Pie	12,697	$1.75	186%	December 20, 2001
Chocolate Sponge	9234	$0.75	300%	November 20, 2001

● The Excel worksheet column letters and row numbers are not shown in Print Preview. However, these will be needed in the printed version. Also, as the shape of the table is rectangular, it would be better positioned on the page in landscape orientation rather than in portrait, as it is at present. We'll use the options in **Setup** to make these changes to our table.

2 PAGE SETUP

● Click on **Setup** at the top of the window.

● The **Page Setup** dialog box opens. Click on the **Page** tab at the top of this dialog box if it is not already available.

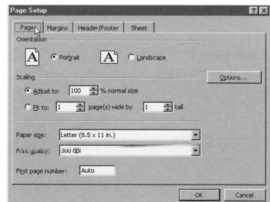

3 PAGE ORIENTATION

● You can see in the top part of the window, that the orientation is set to the default **Portrait**.

● To change the page orientation, click on the **Landscape** radio button.

● Click on **OK** at the foot of the window and you are returned to the **Print Preview** screen where the table is shown in landscape orientation when you zoom out.

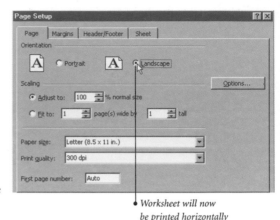

● *Worksheet will now be printed horizontally*

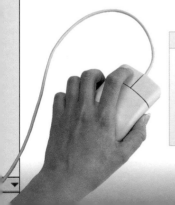

SOUTH LODGE HOTEL DESSERTS				
Dessert name	**Desserts sold**	**Cost per dessert**	**% profit**	**Date next costed**
Blackberry & Apple Crumble	11245	$0.75	500%	April 1, 2000
Banoffee Pie	10541	$1.00	450%	May 1, 2000
Fresh Fruit Salad	22341	$1.50	700%	April 2, 2000
Pecan Pie	12897	$1.75	186%	December 20, 2001
Chocolate Sponge	9234	$0.75	300%	November 20, 2001

GRIDLINES

Excel 2000 will only print gridlines when there is no background color. If your table needs to have gridlines it must be in black and white. You can set the gridlines on by clicking on the **Gridlines** tick box in the **Print options** on the **Sheet** tab of the **Page Setup** window we have just used.

4 COLUMN AND ROW HEADINGS

● The column letters and row numbers can now be added so that the table has the appearance that it has on the Excel worksheet. Click on **Setup** again and the **Page Setup** dialog box appears as before

● Click on the **Sheet** tab at the top of the window.

● In the **Print** section in the center of the box, click on the check box next to **Row and column headings**.

● Click on **OK**. Now we can see that column letters A to E and row numbers 1 to 10 have been added to our table to be printed.

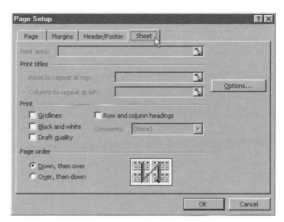

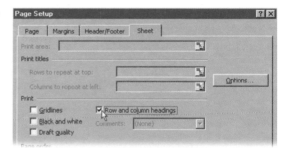

● *Column letters added to table*

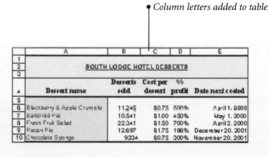

	A	B	C	D	E
1					
2		SOUTH LODGE HOTEL DESSERTS			
3					
4	Dessert name	Desserts sold	Cost per dessert	% profit	Date next costed
5					
6	Blackberry & Apple Crumble	11,245	$0.75	500%	April 1, 2000
7	Banana Pie	10,541	$1.00	450%	May 1, 2000
8	Fresh Fruit Salad	22,341	$1.50	700%	April 2, 2000
9	Pecan Pie	12,697	$1.75	166%	December 20, 2001
10	Chocolate Sponge	9,234	$0.75	300%	November 20, 2001

5 POSITIONING THE TABLE

● Currently the table is in the upper left-hand corner of the page, but would look better in the center, and larger to fill more of the page. Click on **Setup** and click on the **Margins** tab.

● Toward the foot of the box is a **Center on page** section. Click in each of the two check boxes, **Horizontally** and **Vertically**.

● Click on **OK** and the table is now positioned in the center of the page.

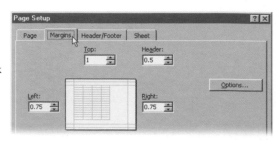

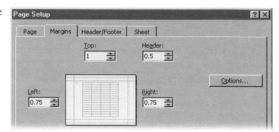

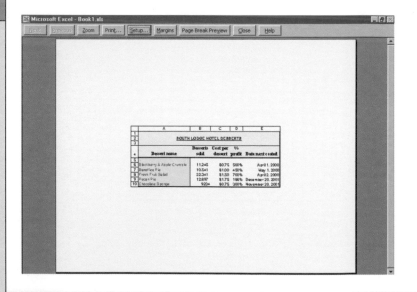

6 PAGE-FITTING THE TABLE

● To fit the table to the page, click on **Setup** at the top of the window and click on the **Page** tab.

● In the center of the box there is a **Scaling** section where the table can be adjusted to a percentage of the normal size. It is currently set to 100%. Increase the size to 150% by clicking the top spin button.

● Click **OK** at the foot of the window. The table has been resized and now fits well on the page.

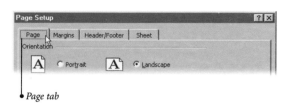

Page tab

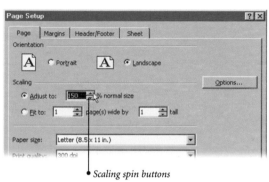

Scaling spin buttons

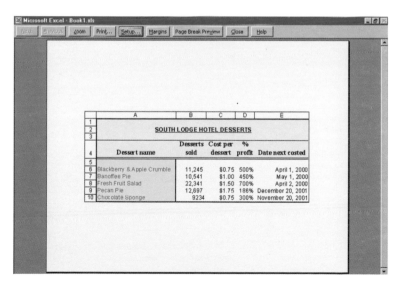

7 HEADERS AND FOOTERS

● Headers and footers are a useful means of adding information to a table. Click on **Setup** and click on the **Header/Footer** tab.

● The **Custom Header** and **Custom Footer** buttons enable headers and footers to be set up quickly. Click on **Custom Header** and the **Header** dialog box opens. The insertion point is positioned automatically in the left-hand box on the screen. We'll use this box to hold the page title.

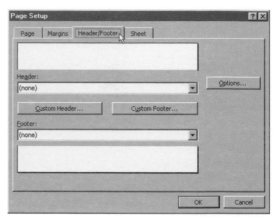

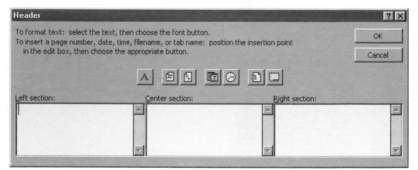

● Enter **South Lodge Hotel Desserts Table**.

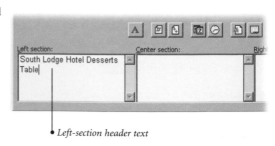

● Left-section header text

● As this is the page title, the text can be increased in size and made bold. Highlight the text **South Lodge Hotel Desserts Table**. Click on the **Font** button, which is the one with a blue capital **A**.

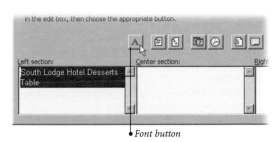

● *Font button*

● The **Font** dialog box appears. Click on the Font style **Bold**. Scroll down the size list and click on Size **14**. Click on the down arrow next to the **Underline** box and choose **Double**, and then click on **OK** at the foot of the window.

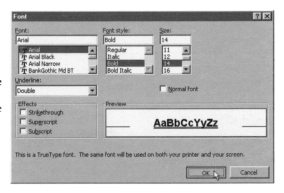

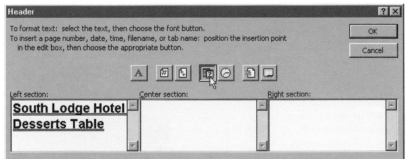

● The **Header** dialog box reappears where, for example, today's date can be inserted into the right section of the Header. Click in the right section and the insertion point is automatically positioned on the extreme right of the box. Click on the button that shows **7** and **8** on it and looks like a calendar.

● The text **&[Date]** appears in the box and indicates that today's date will be inserted into the header and printed on the page. Click on **OK**.

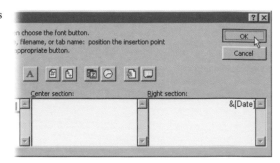

● You are returned to the **Page Setup** dialog box. Click on **Custom Footer**.

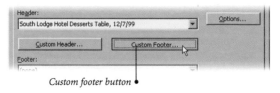

Custom footer button ●

● The insertion point is automatically positioned in the left-hand box of the screen. This box will be used to hold the page number. Click on the button with a single hash sign on it.

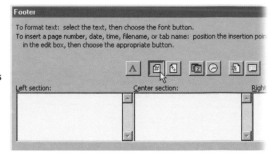

● The text **&[Page]** appears in the box indicating that the page number will be printed on the page footer.

Page ranges
If you have several pages of tables, you can set up pages as, for example, Page 1 of 4, by clicking on the **Headers and Footers** button with two plus signs instead of the single hash sign as used in our working example.

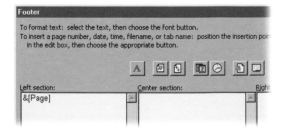

● Click in the right-hand box. This box will be used to show the Excel file name. Click on the icon with the green Excel X on it.

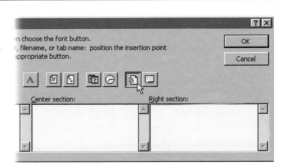

● The text &[**File**] is displayed and this is where the Excel file name will be printed on the page footer.
● Click on **OK** at the top of the dialog box. Click on **OK** at the foot of the **Page Setup** dialog box, and the table is ready to print. Click on **Close** to close the Print Preview window.

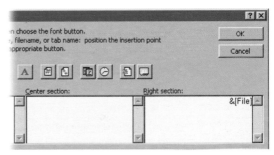

Close button ●

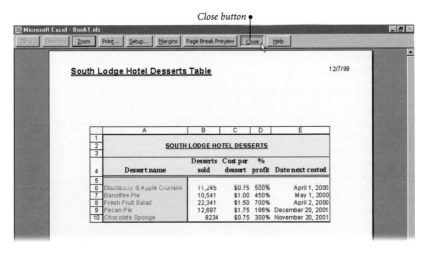

PRINTING THE PAGE

As we have seen by using Print Preview, we now have the page
in the format we wish to print. In Excel the printing of the page
is very similar to printing in other Microsoft Office programs.

CHOOSING THE PRINT OPTIONS

The method of printing a number of
copies and the collation of the copies is
the same as all Office programs. The only
two differences found in Excel are the
options to print the active sheet or the
entire workbook, which are covered here.

1 PRINTING A SINGLE COPY

● Click on **File** in the
Menu bar and select **Print**.
● The **Print** dialog box
opens. The default settings
can be accepted here
because only one copy of
the table needs to be
printed to check its
appearance.
● Click on **OK** at the foot
of the dialog box and the
Excel table is printed.

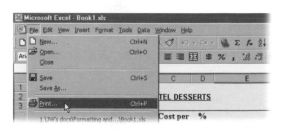

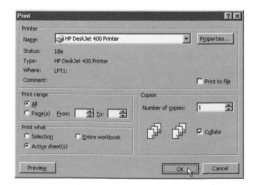

2 PRINTING A SELECTION

● Select the cells A1 to E8.
● Open the **Print** dialog box (see opposite).

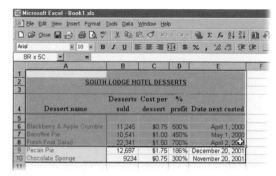

● In the bottom left-hand corner of the **Print** dialog box there is a section labeled **Print what**. The first option is **Selection**, which prints a selected part of the worksheet. Click on **Selection**.
● Rather than wasting paper by printing this selection, it can first be viewed using Print Preview. Click on the **Preview** button at the bottom left of the window.

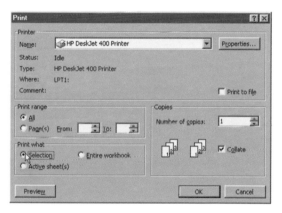

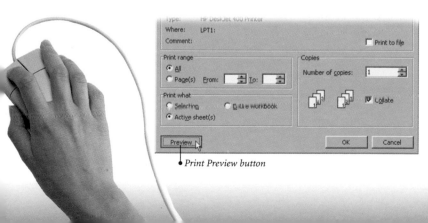

● Print Preview button

● Only the selected cells
are visible in the Preview
window.

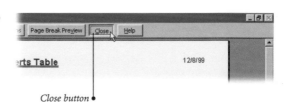

● Click on **Close** at the top
of the screen.

Close button

3 PRINTING THE ACTIVE SHEET

● Now let's look at the
default option **Active
sheet(s)**. The active sheet is
the worksheet that you are
currently working on.

● Click on **File** and then
Print as before. Notice that
the default Active sheet has
been reset automatically.

● Click on **Preview** and
you can see that now the
whole table would be
printed.

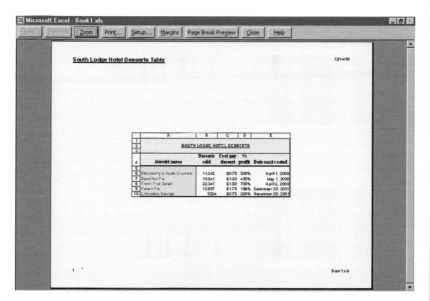

● Click on **Close** at the top
of the screen to return to
the Excel worksheet
● Open the **Print** dialog
box again. The last option
is to print the **Entire
Workbook**. This is very
useful when you have many
sheets of data in an Excel
workbook which all need to
be printed. Rather than
printing each worksheet
individually, you can click
on the **Entire workbook**
option.

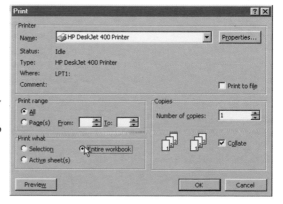

THE PRINT AREA

Excel allows you to change the area to be printed, and you can easily alter the print page breaks. This section covers the main ways to manipulate the area of the worksheet to be printed.

SETTING THE PRINT AREA

You might need to print several copies of just part of a table, and the easiest way to do this is by setting the Print Area. Let's assume that the South Lodge Hotel accountant is only interested in the dessert details where the date next costed is sometime in the year 2000. In other words, for the moment, the accountant is not interested in the details for the Pecan Pie and Chocolate Sponge desserts.

1 DEFINING THE PRINT AREA

● Select the cells from A1 to E8. Click on **File** on the Menu bar, click on **Print Area** in the drop-down menu and select **Set Print Area** from the submenu.

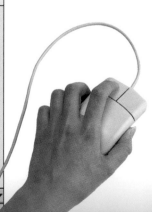

• The print area is now outlined with a dashed line.
• Click on **File** again and select **Print**. Click on **OK** at the foot of the **Print** dialog box and only the cells in the print area are printed.

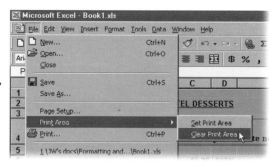

2 CLEARING THE PRINT AREA

• You can clear the print area from the table so that the whole table can be printed again. Click on **File**, followed by **Print Area**, as before and then on **Clear Print Area**.

• Click anywhere on the screen to see that the print area has been deselected.

3 INSERTING PAGE BREAKS

• Assuming that the data is now required in two separate tables we need to insert a page break. Choose the row below where the page break is to occur. In the example, click on row 9, Pecan Pie, so that the page break occurs between Fresh Fruit Salad and Pecan Pie.

● Click on **Insert** on the
Menu bar and then on **Page
Break**.

● A page break will now
have been inserted, but to
check that Page Break is
working we can look at the
table using Page Break
Preview.

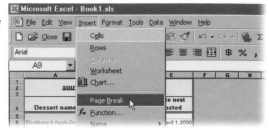

4 VIEWING THE PAGE BREAKS

● To look at the page
breaks, click on **View** on
the Menu bar and then on
Page Break Preview.

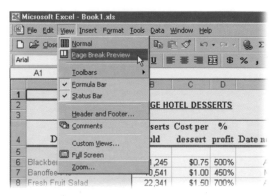

● The **Welcome to Page
Break Preview** message box
is shown center screen.
Click on **OK** and the
message box closes.

● The screen shows the
table greatly reduced, and
two lines highlighting row
9 going from left to right
across the screen. You can
also see the words **Page 1**
superimposed in gray over
the top part of the table.

● Click anywhere on the
screen to deselect the page
break.

● You can now see a bright blue line between **Fresh Fruit Salad** and **Pecan Pie**, which shows where the page break has been inserted.

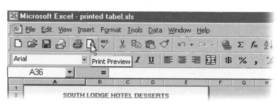

5 PREVIEWING THE PRINTED PAGES

● To see what the two tables will look like when printed, click on the **Print Preview** button, and page 1 of the table is displayed, showing that the last dessert on the page is Fresh Fruit Salad.

● To view page 2, position the mouse cursor on the lower part of the vertical scroll bar and click once. (Alternatively, click on **Next** at the top left of the Print Preview screen.)

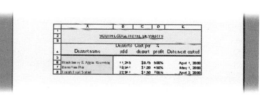

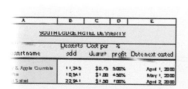

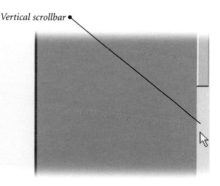

Vertical scrollbar ●

● The new page 2 appears on screen showing the two remaining desserts.

● Click on **Close** at the top of the screen.

● To return to Normal view, click on **View** in the Menu bar and select **Normal**.

● Click off the table when it reappears to clear the blue lines.

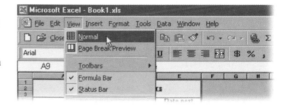

6 REPEATING HEADINGS

● The second table is not very clear without the table title and column headings, but they can be added to the second table.

● Click on **File** on the Menu bar, then on **Page Setup**.

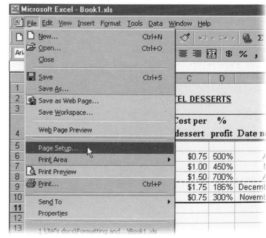

● The **Page Setup** dialog box opens. Click on the **Sheet** tab at the top of the **Page Setup** window.

● To repeat the table heading and column labels on every page, the range of cells that they occupy needs to be identified. A cell range consists of a dollar sign, the first cell address, a colon, a second dollar sign, and the last cell address in the range. For example, a range might be expressed as $A3:$F7.

● Under the **Print titles** section of the **Sheet** tab, the first option is **Rows to repeat at top**, which is what is required for the second table.

● Click in the extreme right-hand side of the **Rows to repeat at top** box where there is a small red arrow, known as a *dialog collapse* box.

● The **Page Setup - Rows to repeat at top:** text box opens on top of the worksheet so that it is easy to see the range of cells to be repeated.

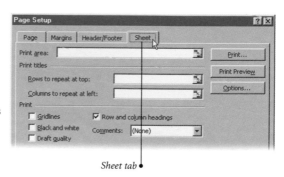

Sheet tab ●

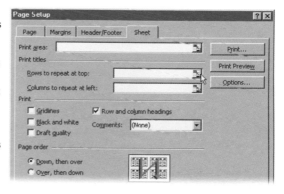

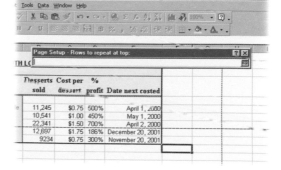

Desserts sold	Cost per dessert	% profit	Date next costed
11,245	$0.75	500%	April 1, 2000
10,541	$1.00	450%	May 1, 2000
22,341	$1.50	700%	April 1, 2000
12,697	$1.75	186%	December 20, 2001
9234	$0.75	300%	November 20, 2001

● The range of cells we
need to be repeated on
every page is from cell A1
to cell E4, so enter **$A1:$E4**
in the text box and click on
the **x** close button at the
top right corner of the box.

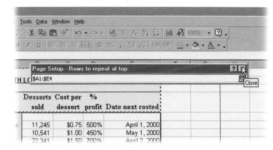

● You are returned to the
Sheet window. Now click
on **OK** at the foot of the
window.

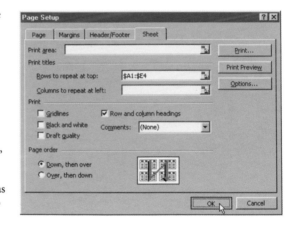

● To see the second table,
click on **Print Preview** 📄
and the first table is
displayed on the screen, as
before. Click on **Zoom** to
see the text more clearly.

	A	B	C	D	E
1					
2	**SOUTH LODGE HOTEL DESSERTS**				
3					
4	**Dessert name**	Desserts sold	Cost per dessert	% profit	Date next costed
5					
6	Blackberry & Apple Crumble	11,245	$0.75	500%	April 1, 2000
7	Banoffee Pie	10,541	$1.00	450%	May 1, 2000
8	Fresh Fruit Salad	22,341	$1.50	700%	April 2, 2000

● Click on **Next** at the top of the screen to view the second table.

● You can see that the second table now includes the title and column headings, the same as in the first table. Both tables can now be printed.

7 PRINTING THE FINAL TABLES

● Click on **Close** at the top of the screen, click on **File**, then on **Print**, and click on **OK** at the bottom of the **Print** dialog box.

● Both tables are now printed.

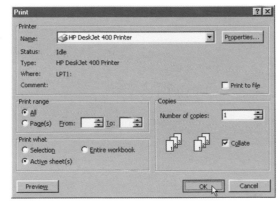

Vertical page breaks
If you insert a page break vertically, you will probably need to repeat the columns on the left of the table so that the data still makes sense. For example, if we inserted a

page break in the table, which meant that only the last **Date next costed column** was in a separate table, the first column, **Dessert names**, would also be required so that it was clear which date related to

which dessert. Follow the steps for repeating column headings described above, but insert the range of cells in the **Columns to repeat at left** box on the **Sheet** tab in the **Page Setup** window.

WORDART

WordArt is a Microsoft program that you can use in Excel 2000 as well as in Word 2000. It provides a large variety of sample text styles, any of which you can use on your Excel worksheet to add color and visual impact to your data.

1 THE DRAWING TOOLBAR

Let's explore the use of WordArt using a new worksheet.

● Click on the **Sheet3** tab at the bottom of the screen.

● Click on the Drawing button on the Standard toolbar.

The Drawing toolbar appears at the bottom of your screen.

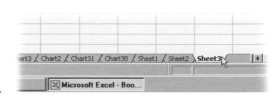

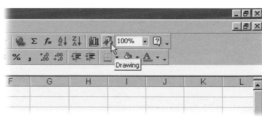

The Drawing toolbar ●

● Click on the **Insert WordArt** icon (shown as a blue capital **A**). The WordArt gallery window appears on your screen showing the 30 predesigned images for you to choose from.

The Insert WordArt icon ●

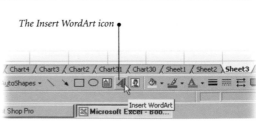

● Click on an image of your choice. In the example we have chosen the multi-colored style.

● Click on **OK** at the bottom of the window. The **Edit WordArt Text** dialog box opens. This allows you to enter the text that you wish to appear on your worksheet in the image you have just chosen. The words **Your Text Here** are already highlighted, so we just have to key in our text.

● Enter your text. In our example, we have entered **WordArt in Excel**.

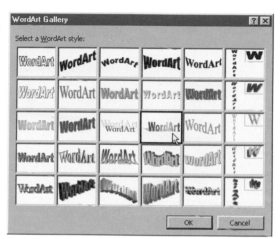

WordArt toolbar
To show the WordArt toolbar, right click on the Standard toolbar and from the drop down list of toolbars, click on WordArt.

● Now we can make other changes to the style of the WordArt. Let's change the font style and size. Click on the down arrow next to the font box and scroll down until you see **Times New Roman** and click on this font style.

● Now click on the down arrow next to the size box, scroll down the list and let's increase the size to **44**.

● Click on **B** to make the text bold.

● Click on **I** to make the text italics.

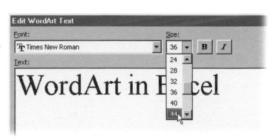

● Click on OK at the bottom of the window.

Selecting text
To carry out any function on WordArt text once it is displayed on the worksheet (see opposite) it needs to be selected. You do this by just holding the mouse pointer over the text until it turns into a four-way black arrow. Click once on the left hand mouse button and the text is selected.

Text Bold ●

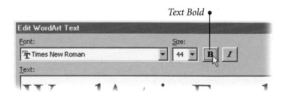

Text Italic ●

• Our WordArt is now displayed on the worksheet. In addition, a new WordArt "floating" toolbar has appeared on the screen. This provides all of the features available to you within WordArt and allows you, for example, to change the text, shape, orientation and color of the WordArt.

• As an example, let's change the shape of our text. Click on the **WordArt Shape** icon.

• Choose a new shape for the text from the menu that appears. In our example we have chosen **Wave 1**.

• The text is now displayed as a wave on the screen.

• Before you can start entering data into the worksheet, you need to exit WordArt by removing the toolbar and deselecting the text. Click on the **✗** close button at the top right of the WordArt floating toolbar, and click anywhere on the worksheet to deselect the text. You can now enter data into the worksheet, as usual.

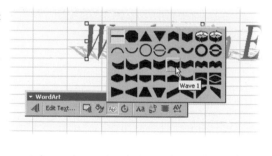

GLOSSARY

ACTIVE CELL
The cell with the thick, black border around it on a worksheet or, in a selected block of cells, the white cell. When you type, the characters appear in the active cell as well as in the Formula bar above the worksheet.

AUTOFIT
AutoFit is used to make the column widths wide enough to show the data entered into the cells in a worksheet.

AUTOFORMAT
AutoFormat is used to format Excel tables of data into predesigned styles.

CELL
A cell is an individual space on the worksheet where the data is entered and stored. The active cell which is bordered in black indicates where the data is being entered.

DIALOG COLLAPSE BOX
This is a button situated at the end of an input box. By clicking on the dialog collapse box, the current dialog box or window is "collapsed" and the user is taken to the original screen. By clicking on the collapse box again, the user is returned to the dialog box. The dialog collapse box thus acts like a switch between one window and another.

FILL
This is the term for the background color or pattern of a cell.

DIALOG BOX
A rectangle that appears on the screen and prompts you for a reply, usually with buttons such as **OK** or **Cancel**.

FLOATING TOOLBAR
This is a toolbar that is not *docked* at the top, bottom, or side of the screen, but *floats* in the main part of the screen.

FONT
Font is the word used to describe the type of text style. The default font in Excel is Arial 12 pt.

FILE
A discrete collection of data stored on the computer.

FORMAT CATEGORY
This is the category or type of format associated with a cell on the Excel worksheet. Categories include General, Number, Date, Time, and Percentage.

GRIDLINES
The gridlines are the vertical and horizontal lines on the worksheet used to create the grid of cells in an Excel worksheet.

HASH SIGN
The hash sign looks like this #. A series of hash signs ####### in a cell in a worksheet indicates that the column is not wide enough to show the input data in full.

ICON
An icon is the name given to the small pictures on any toolbar.

MARQUEE
A border surrounding a selected cell, taking the form of a moving dotted line.

ORIENTATION
This describes the way the page is printed on the sheet of paper. *Portrait* means that the data is printed up and down the page. *Landscape* means that the data is printed horizontally on the page.

PAGE BREAK
A page break shows where the printing on one page ends and the printing on the next page will begin. It is possible to force page breaks in Excel 2000.

PRINT AREA
This is the area of cells that is printed by Excel. Print Areas can be set and cleared by the user.

TOGGLE BUTTONS
A toggle button is any button, that can be "switched" off and on. For example, text can be made bold by clicking on the bold icon (**B**) on the Standard toolbar, and returned to normal by clicking on it again.

WORKBOOK
A workbook is a collection of worksheets. The default Excel workbook has Sheet1, Sheet2, and Sheet3, although other sheets can be added to a workbook.

WORKSHEET
A worksheet is a grid of cells into which the data is entered.

INDEX

ACKNOWLEDGMENTS

PUBLISHER'S ACKNOWLEDGMENTS
Dorling Kindersley would like to thank the following:
Paul Mattock of APM, Brighton, for commissioned photography.
Microsoft Corporation for permission to reproduce screens
from within Microsoft® Excel.

Every effort has been made to trace the copyright holders.
The publisher apologizes for any unintentional omissions and would be pleased,
in such cases, to place an acknowledgment in future editions of this book.

Microsoft® is a registered trademark of Microsoft Corporation
in the United States and/or other countries.